Flower Garden

A Coloring Book for Beautiful Nature

ARK CREATIVE

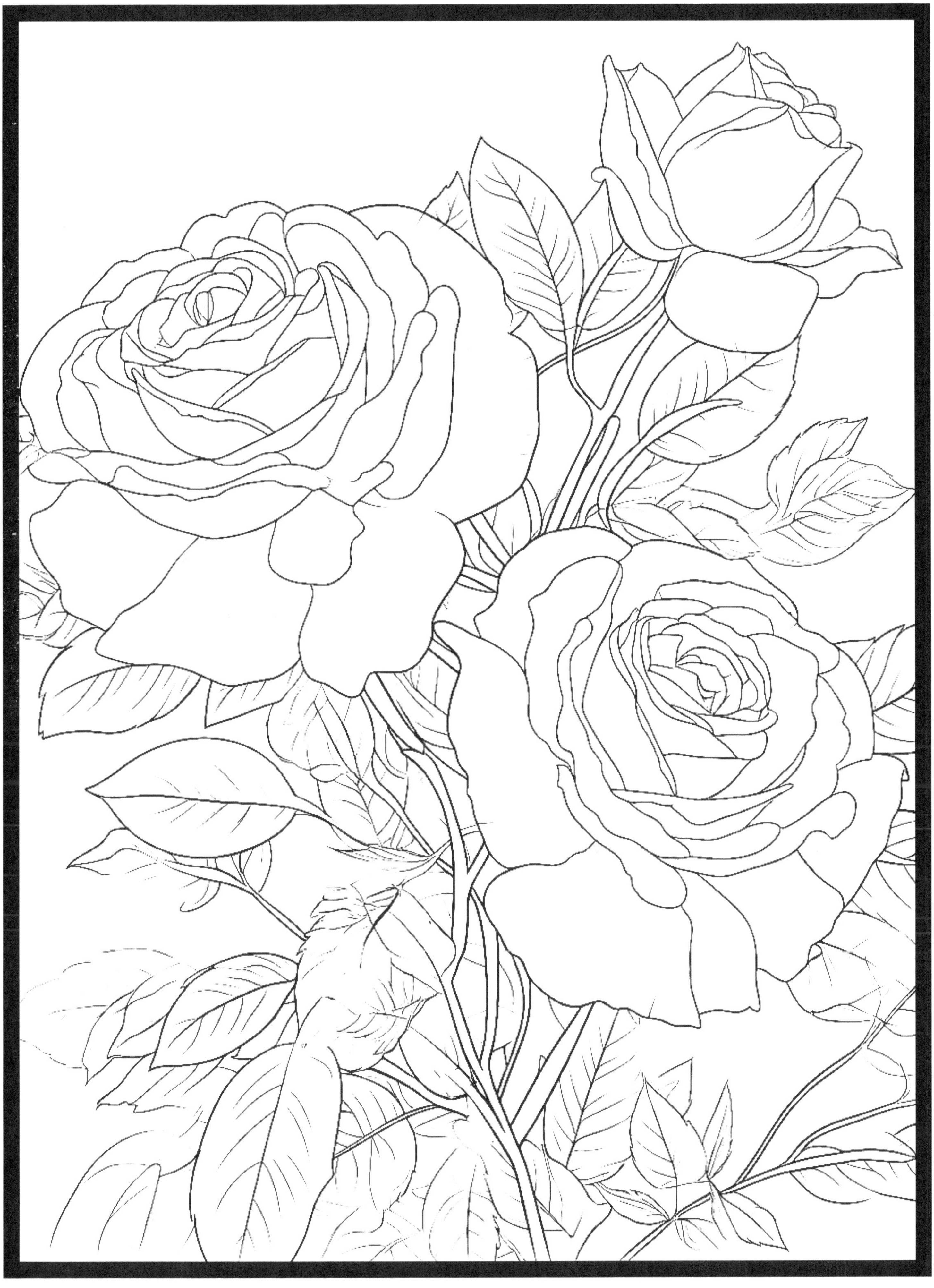

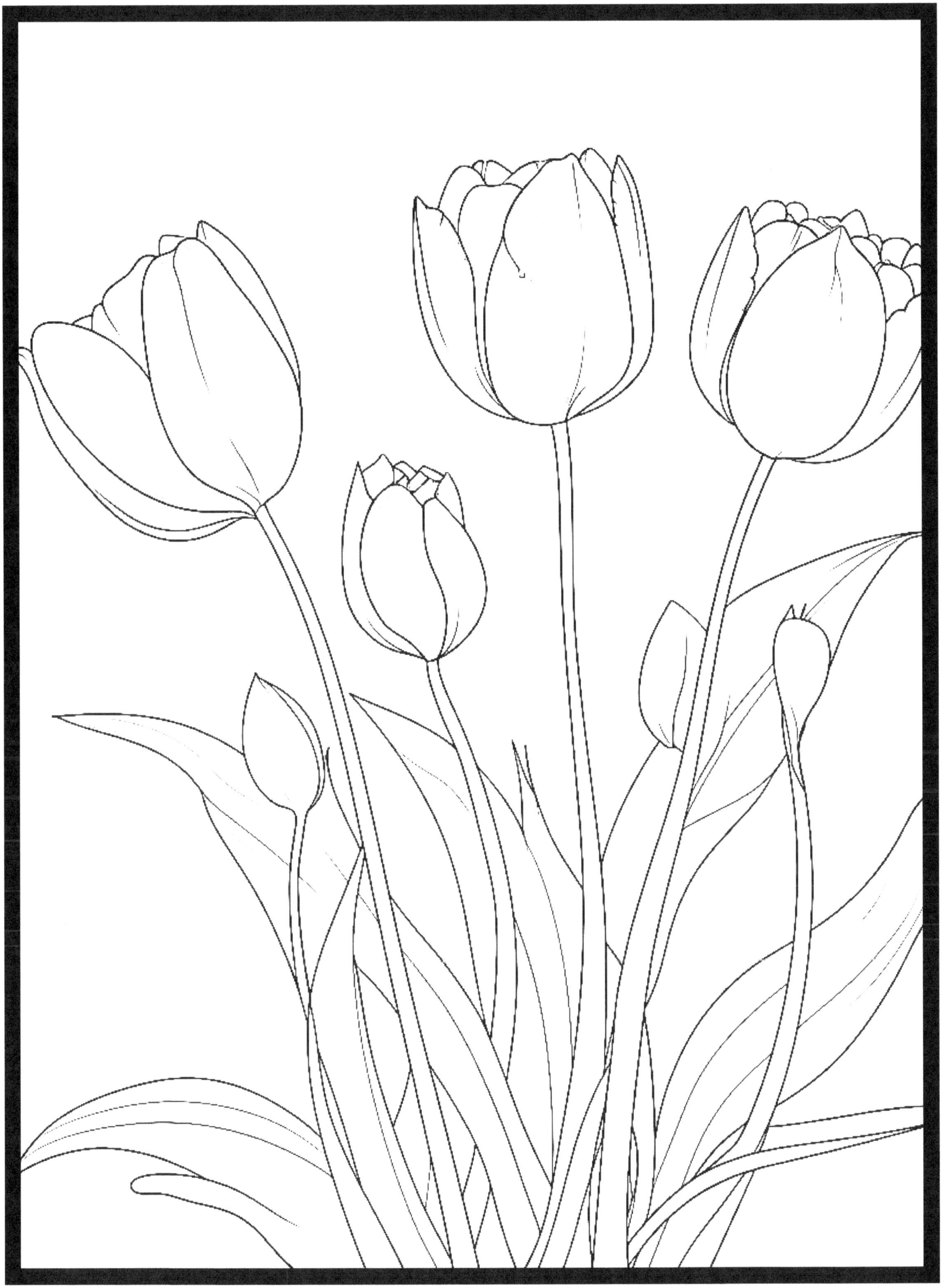

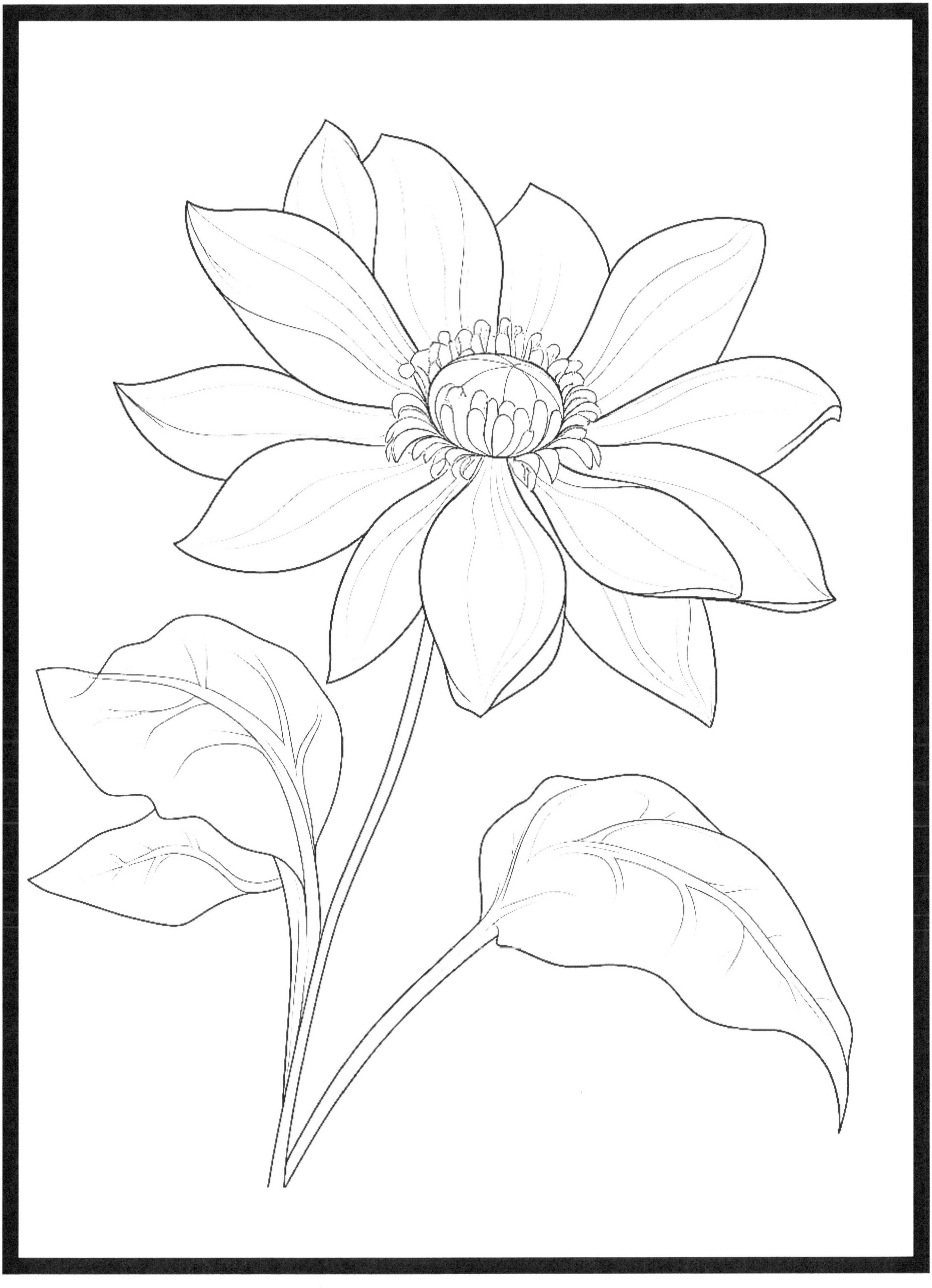

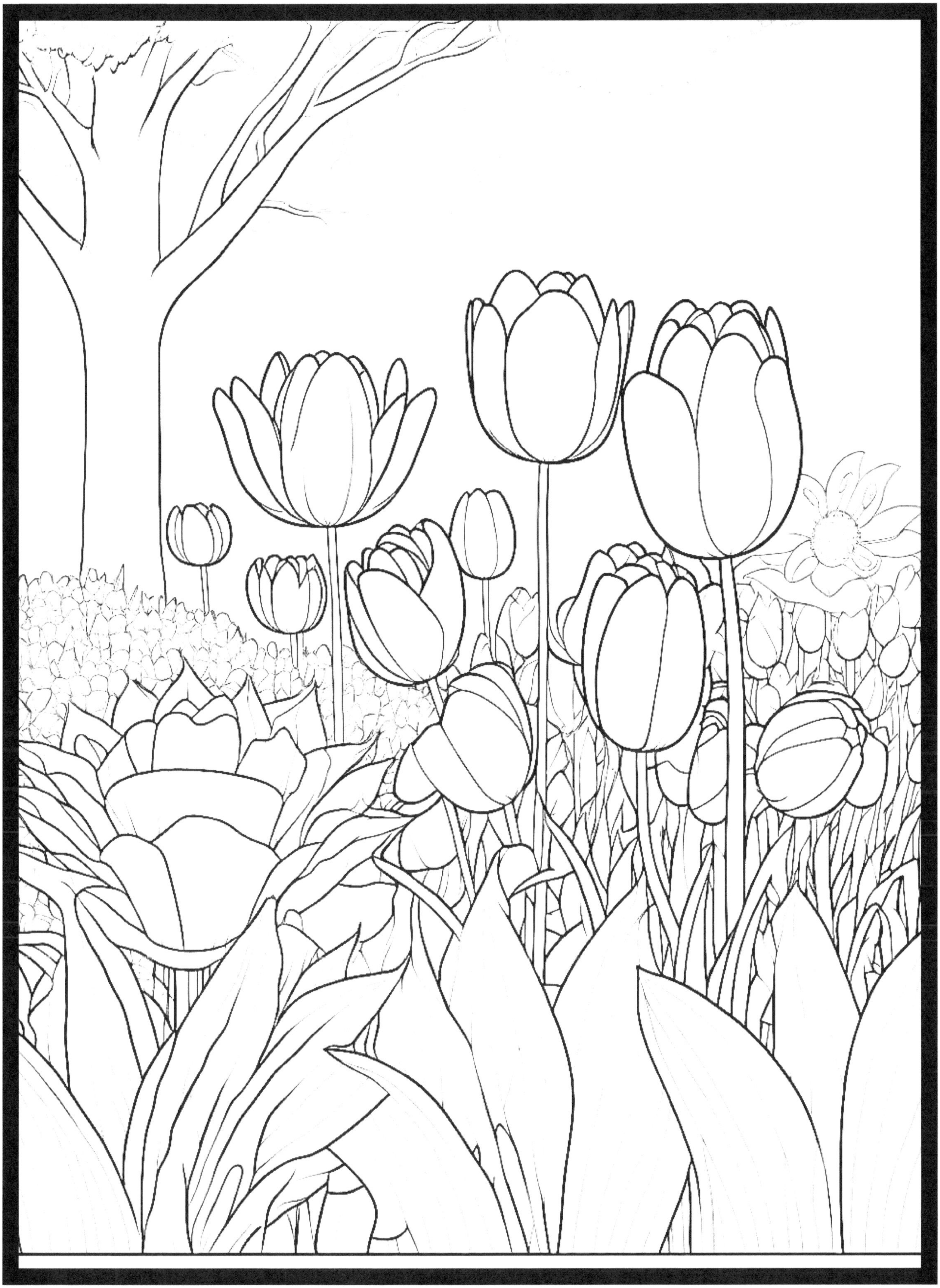

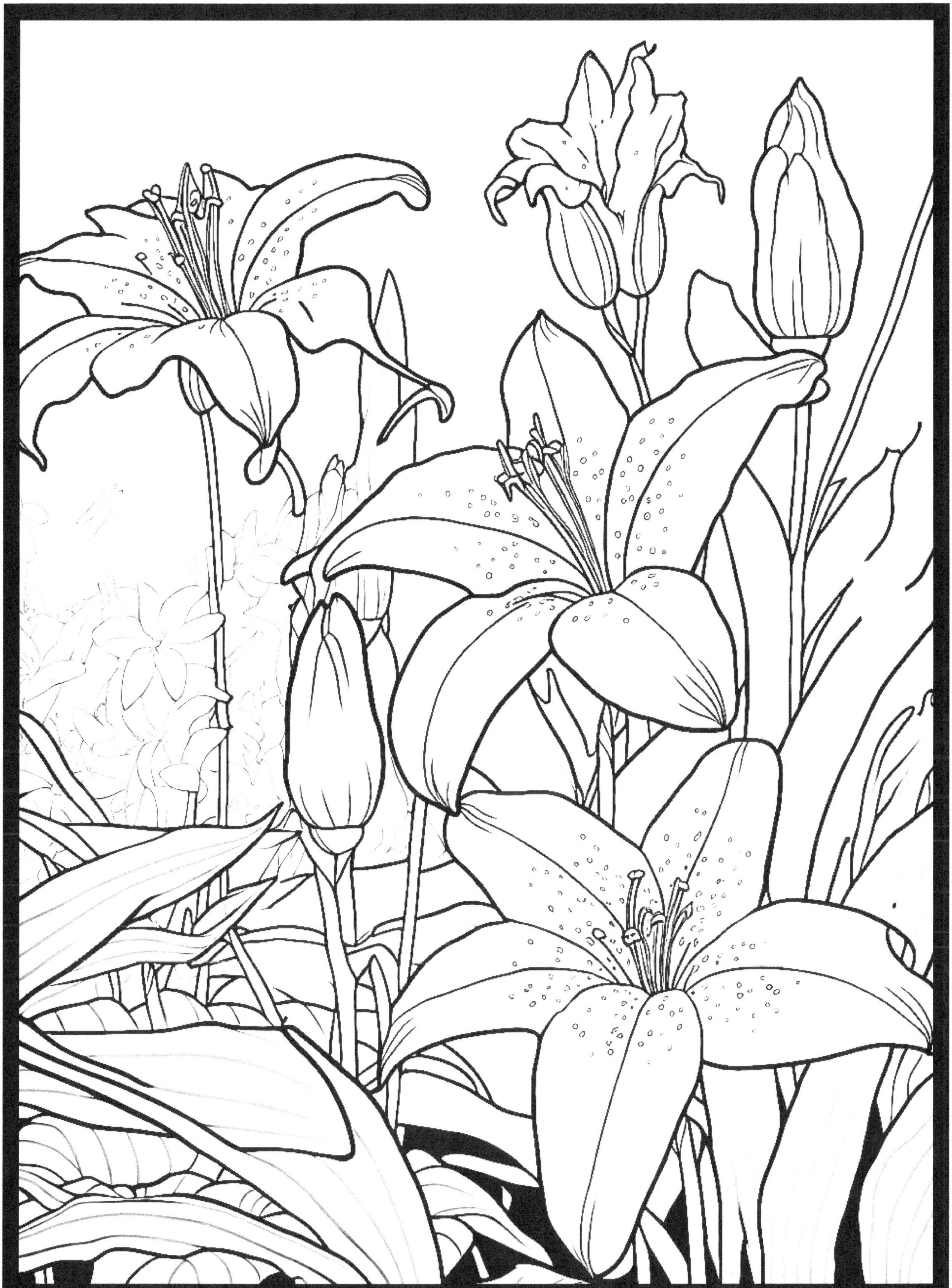

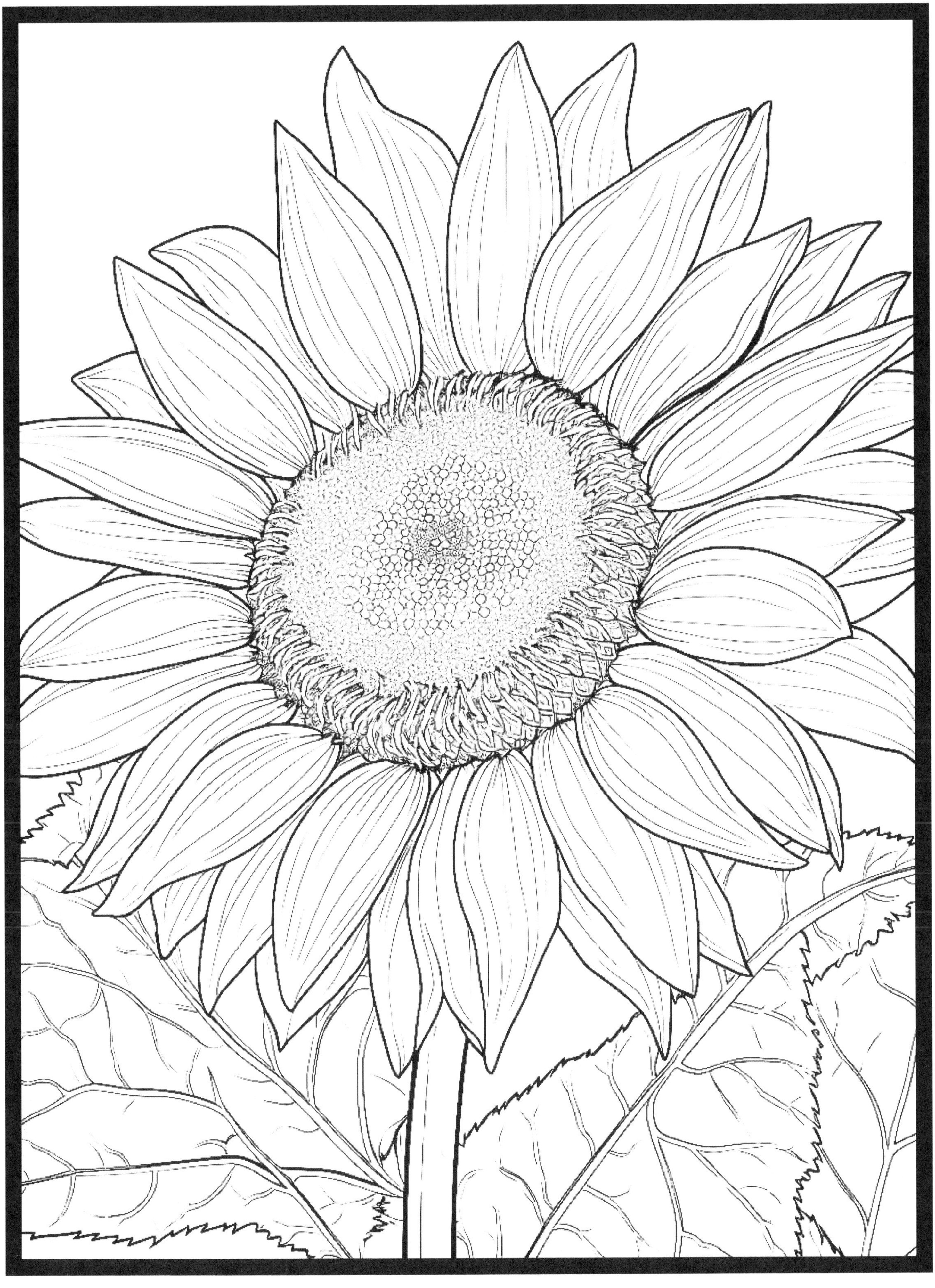

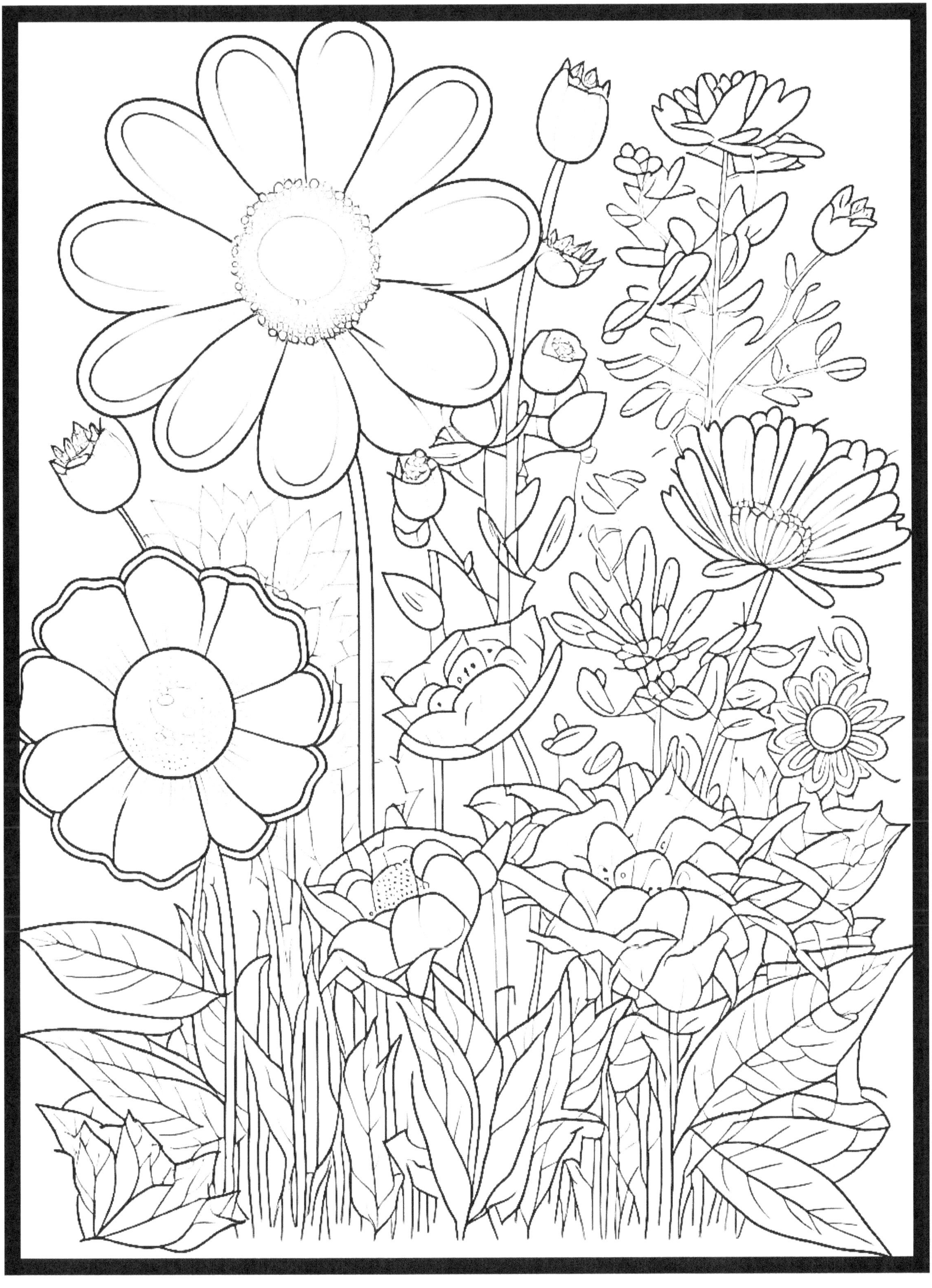

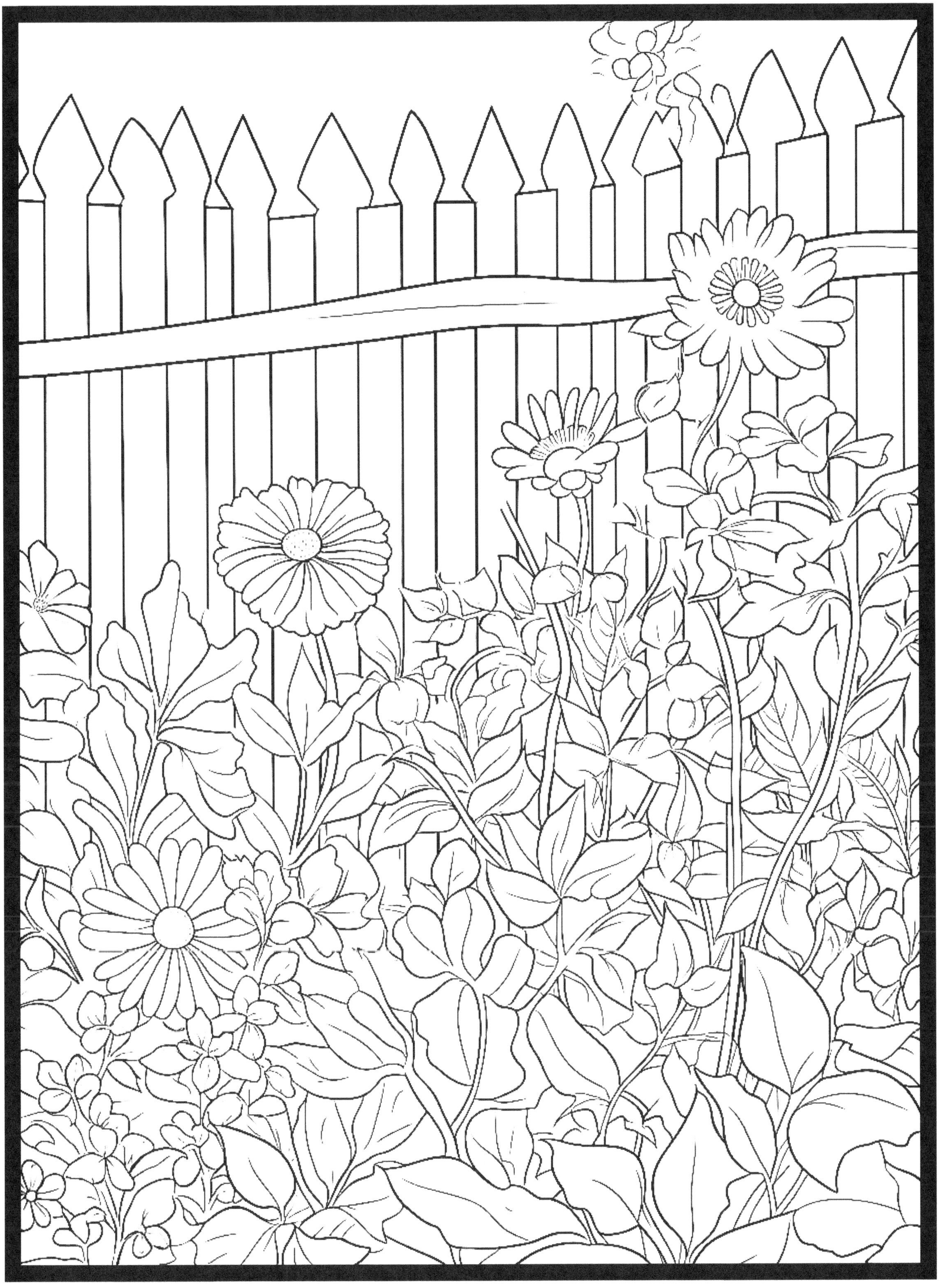

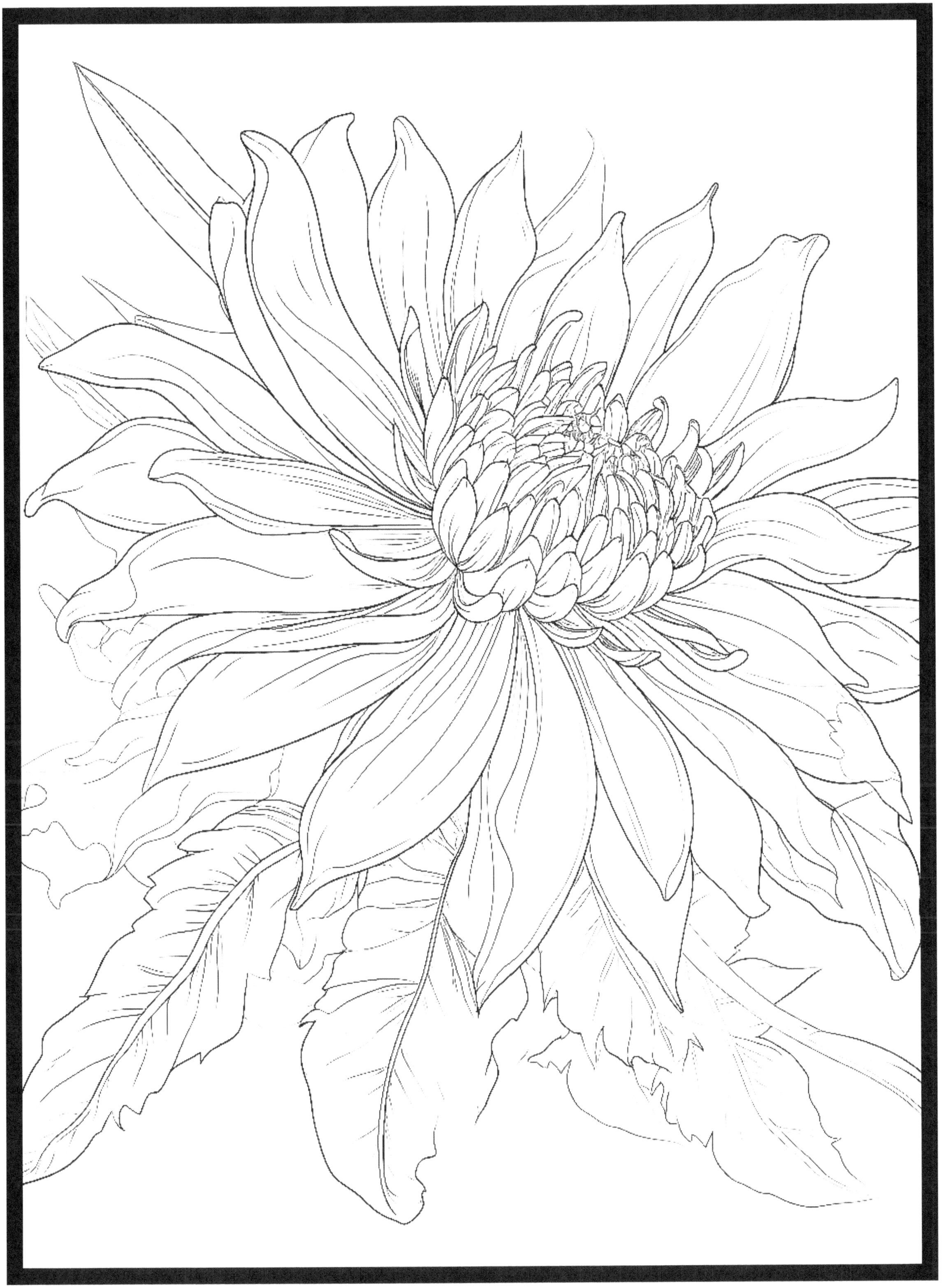

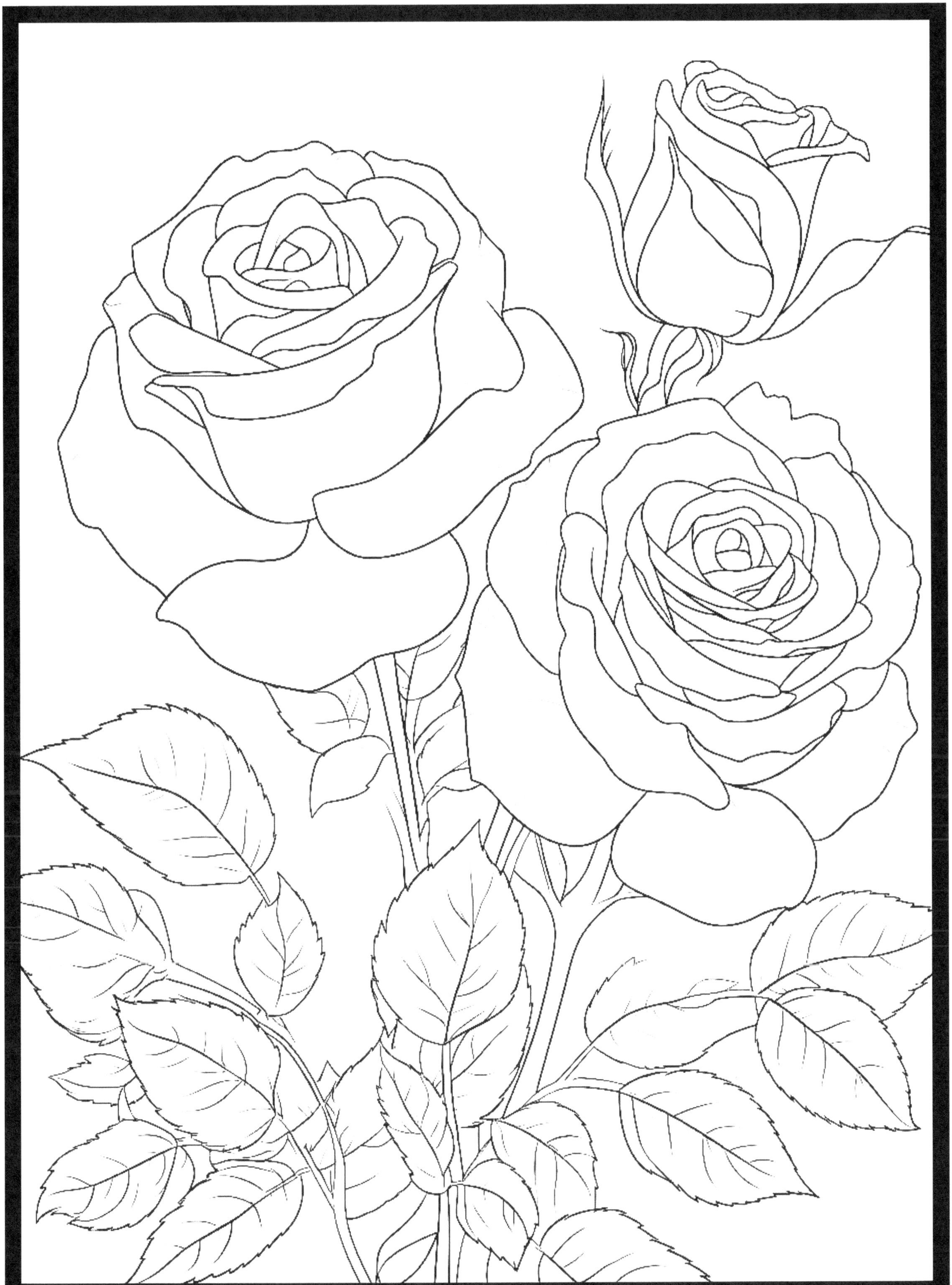

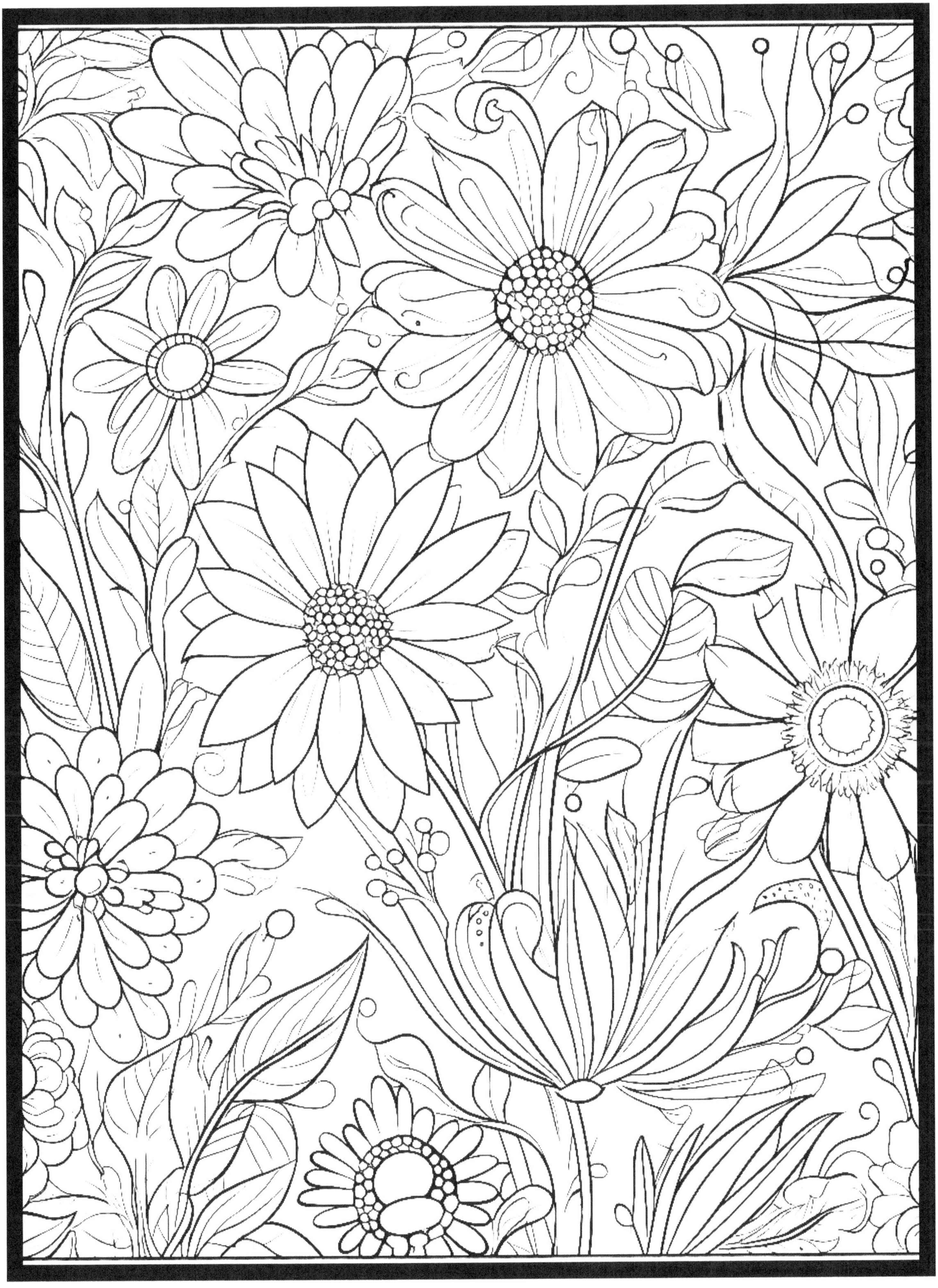

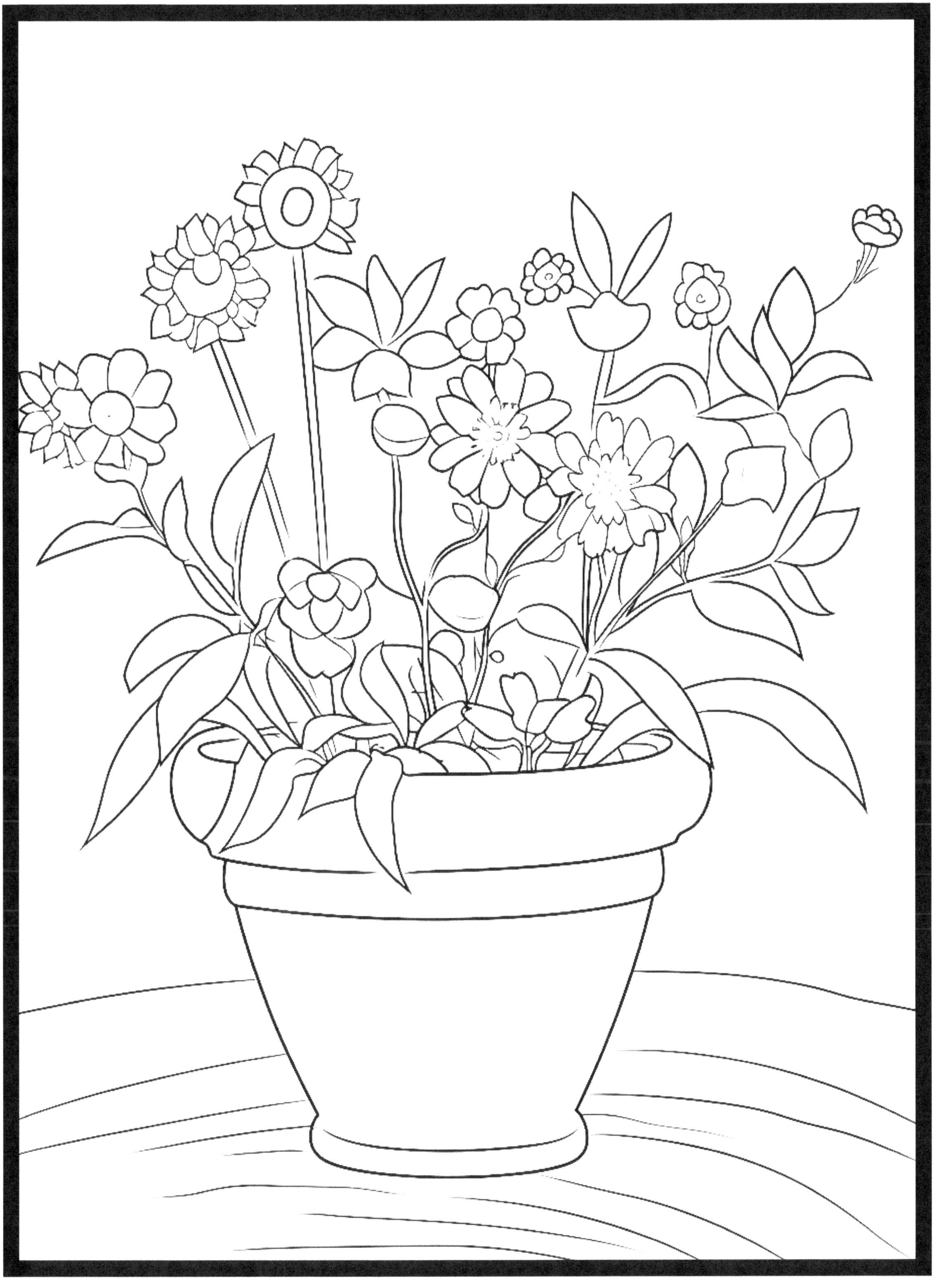

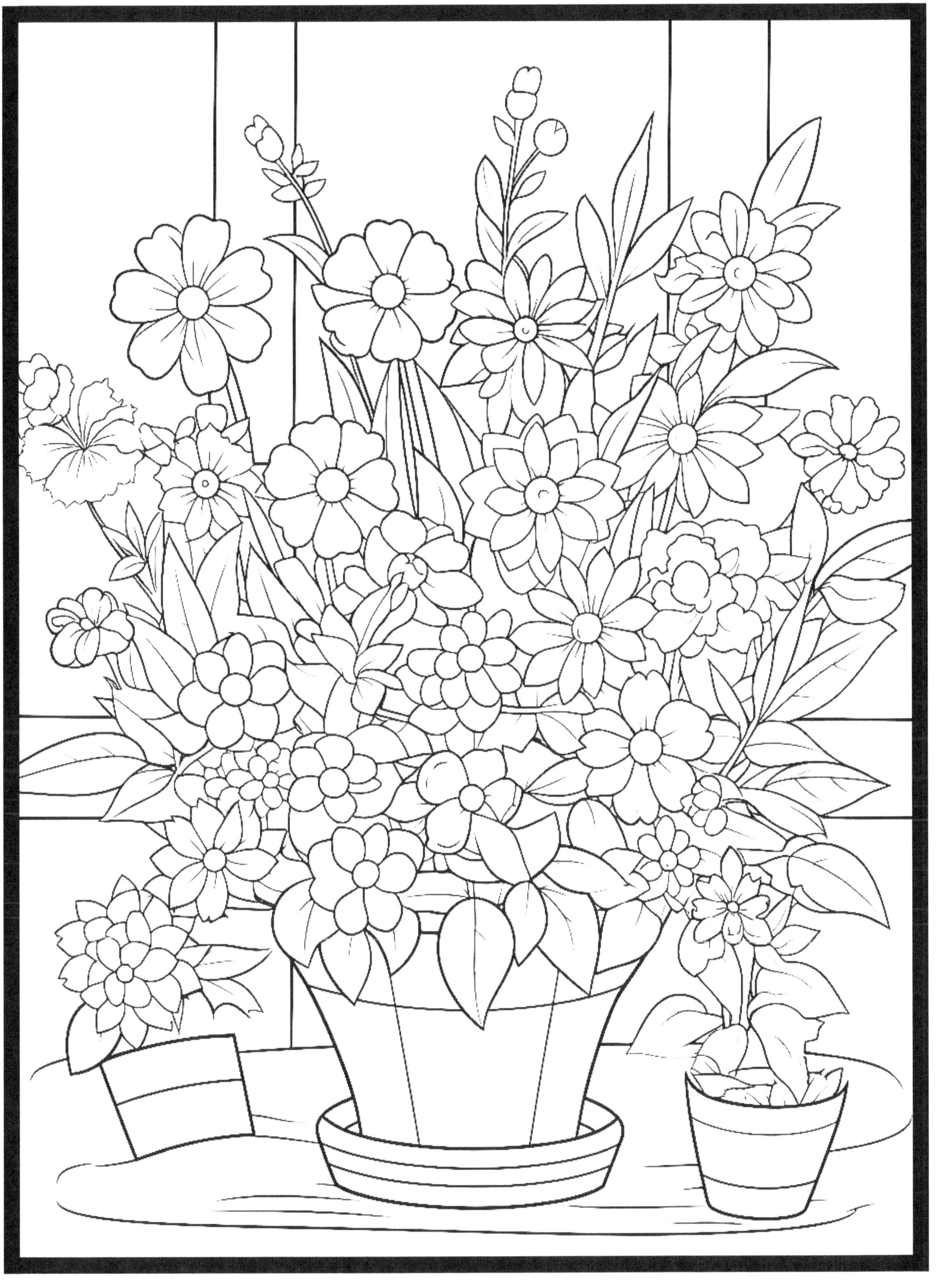

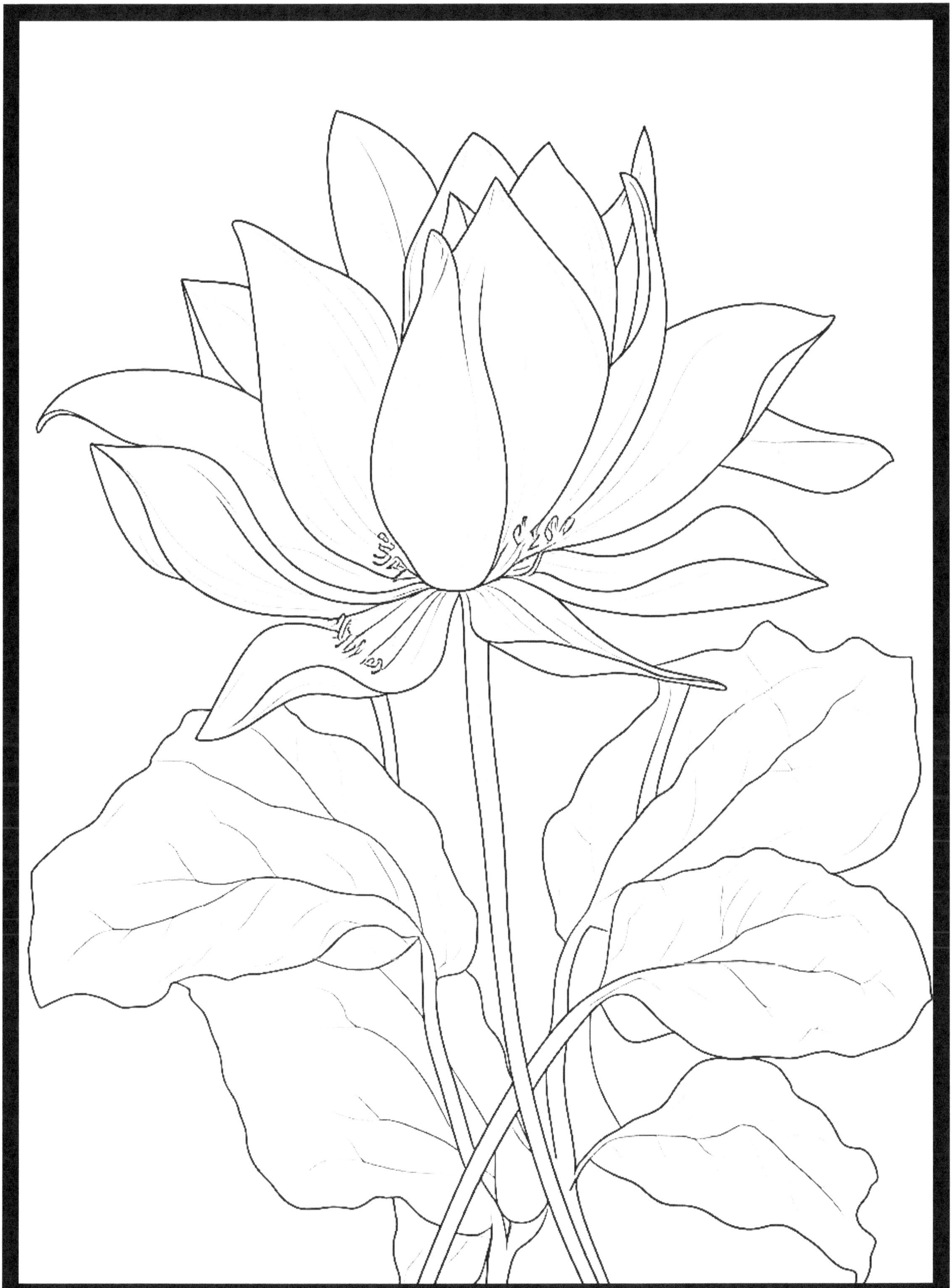

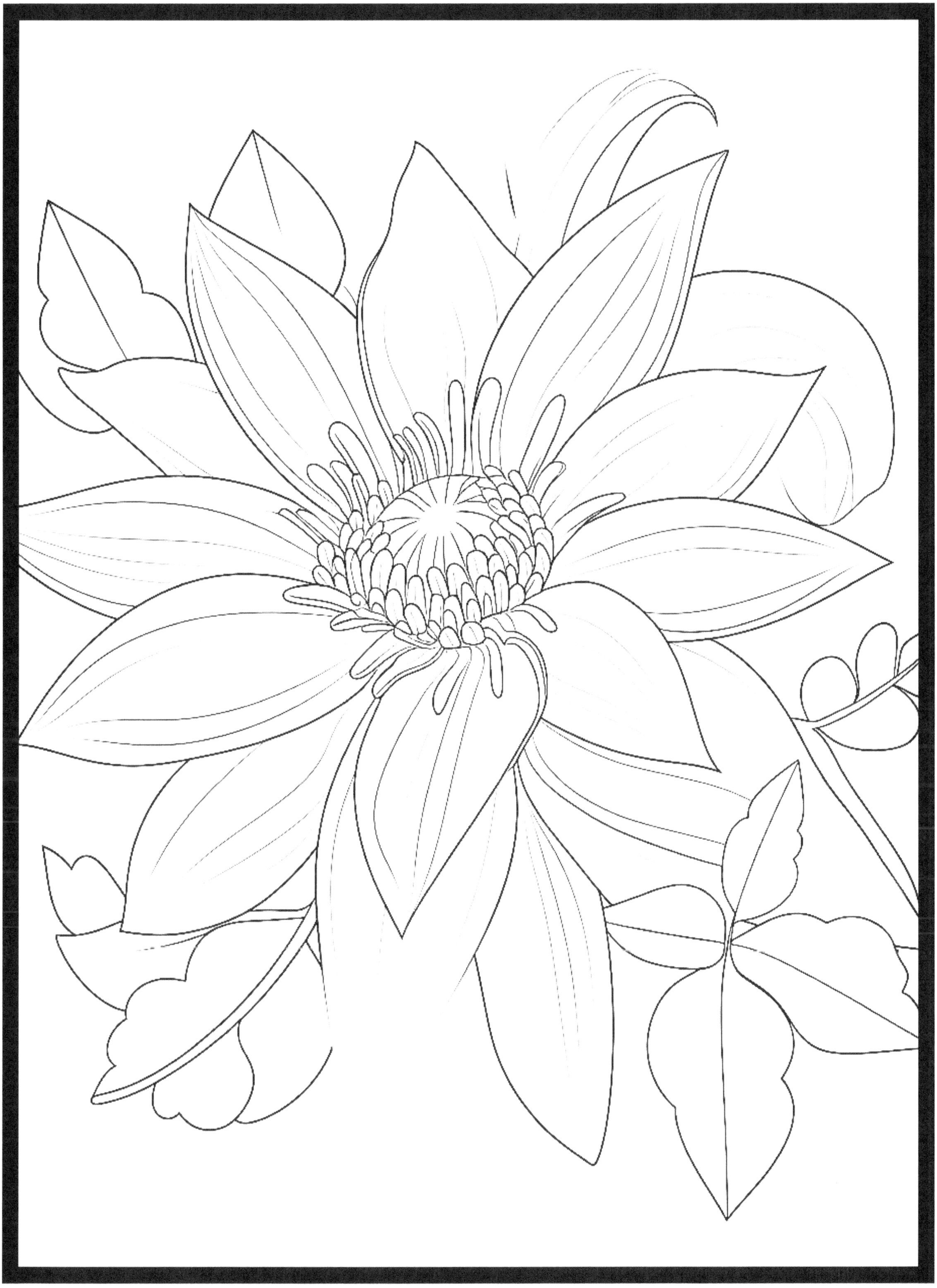

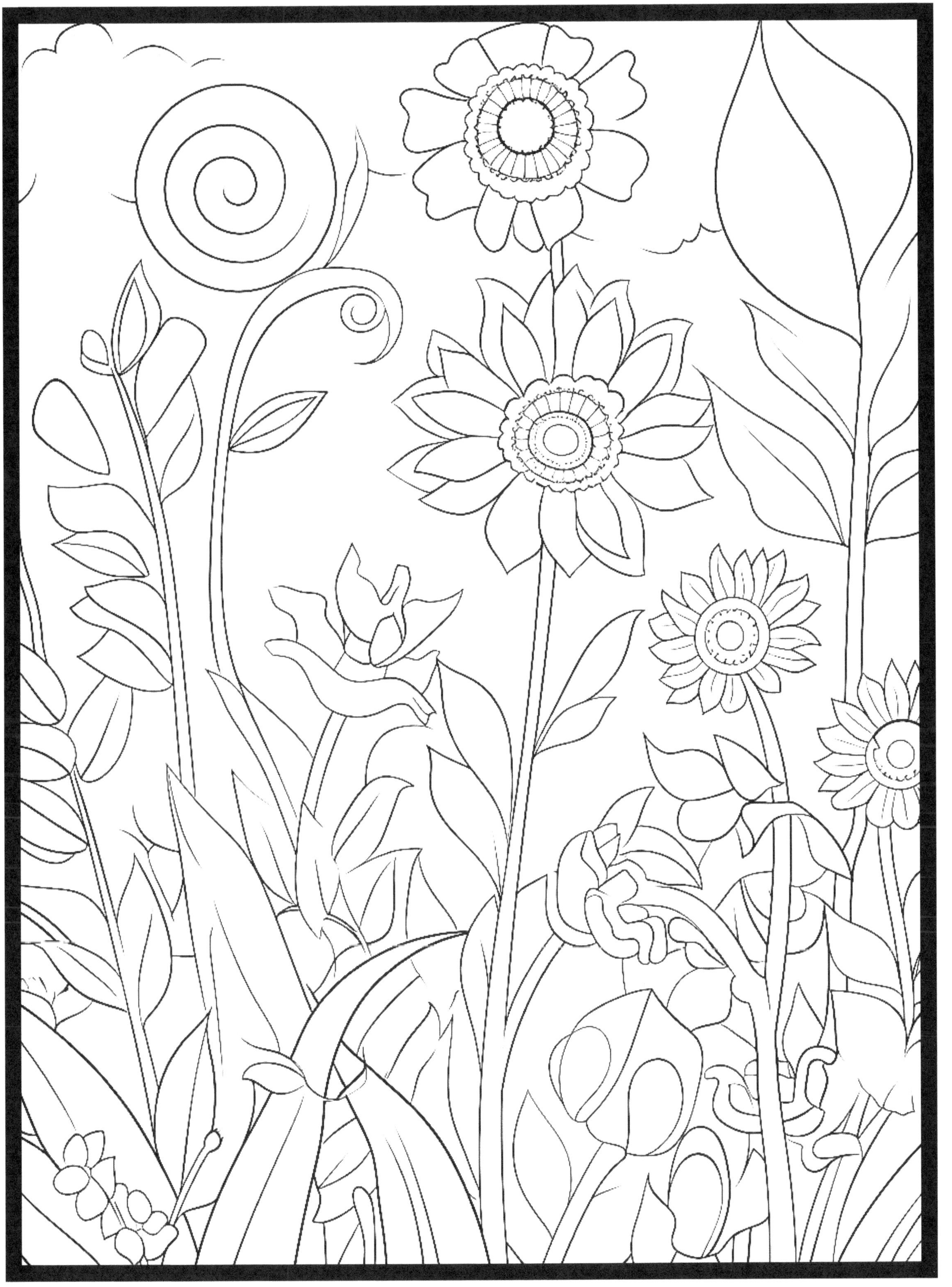

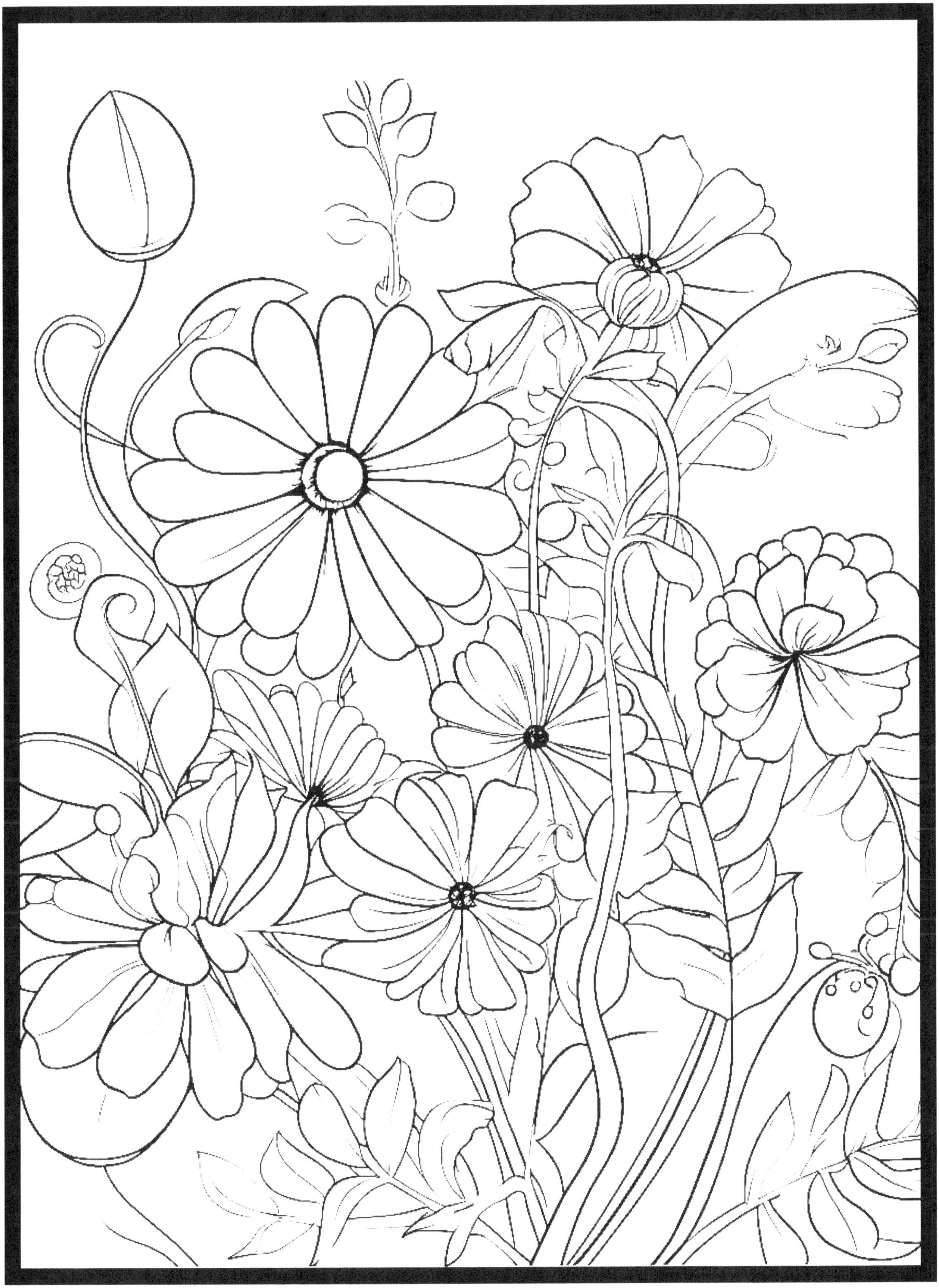

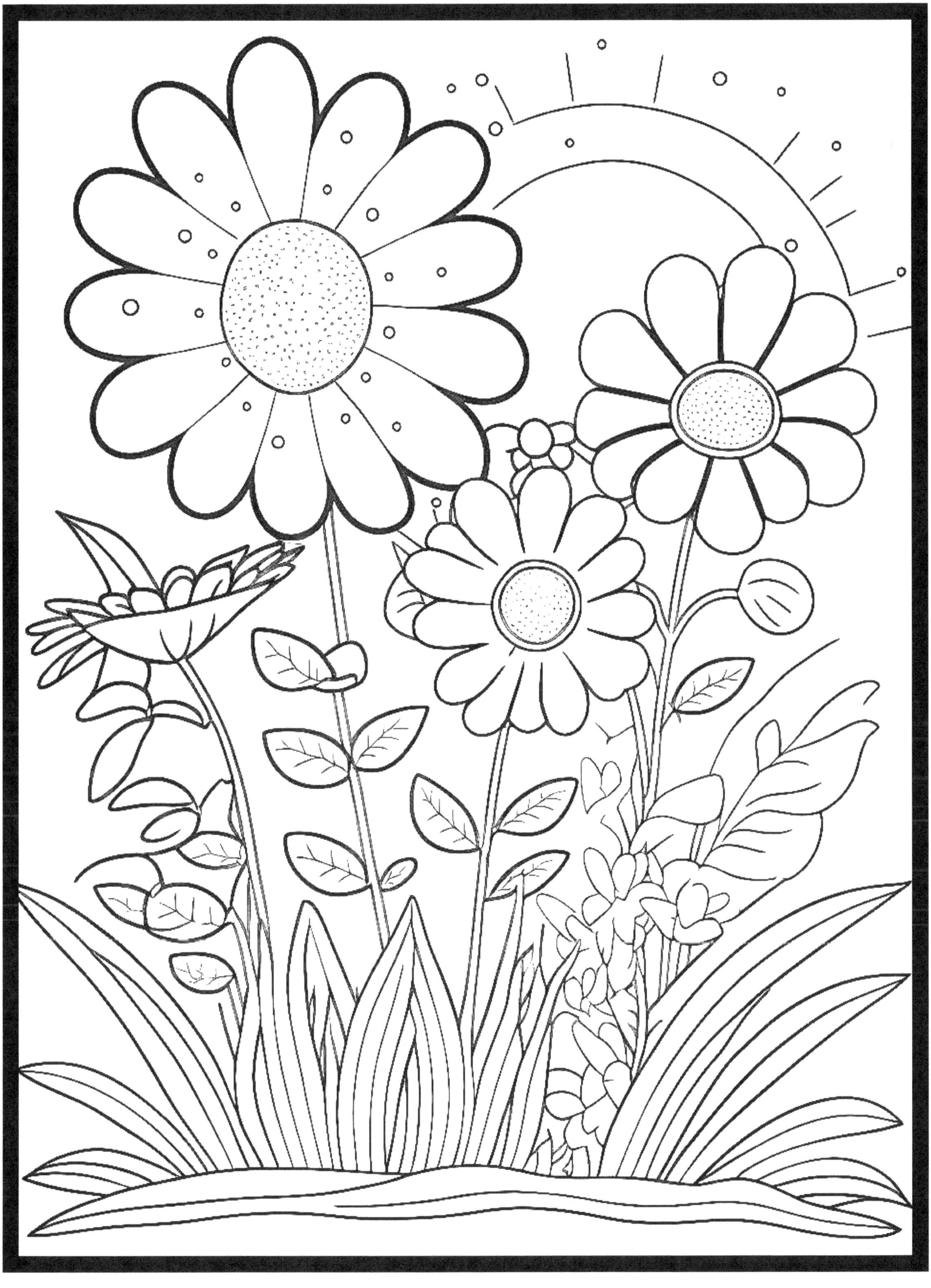

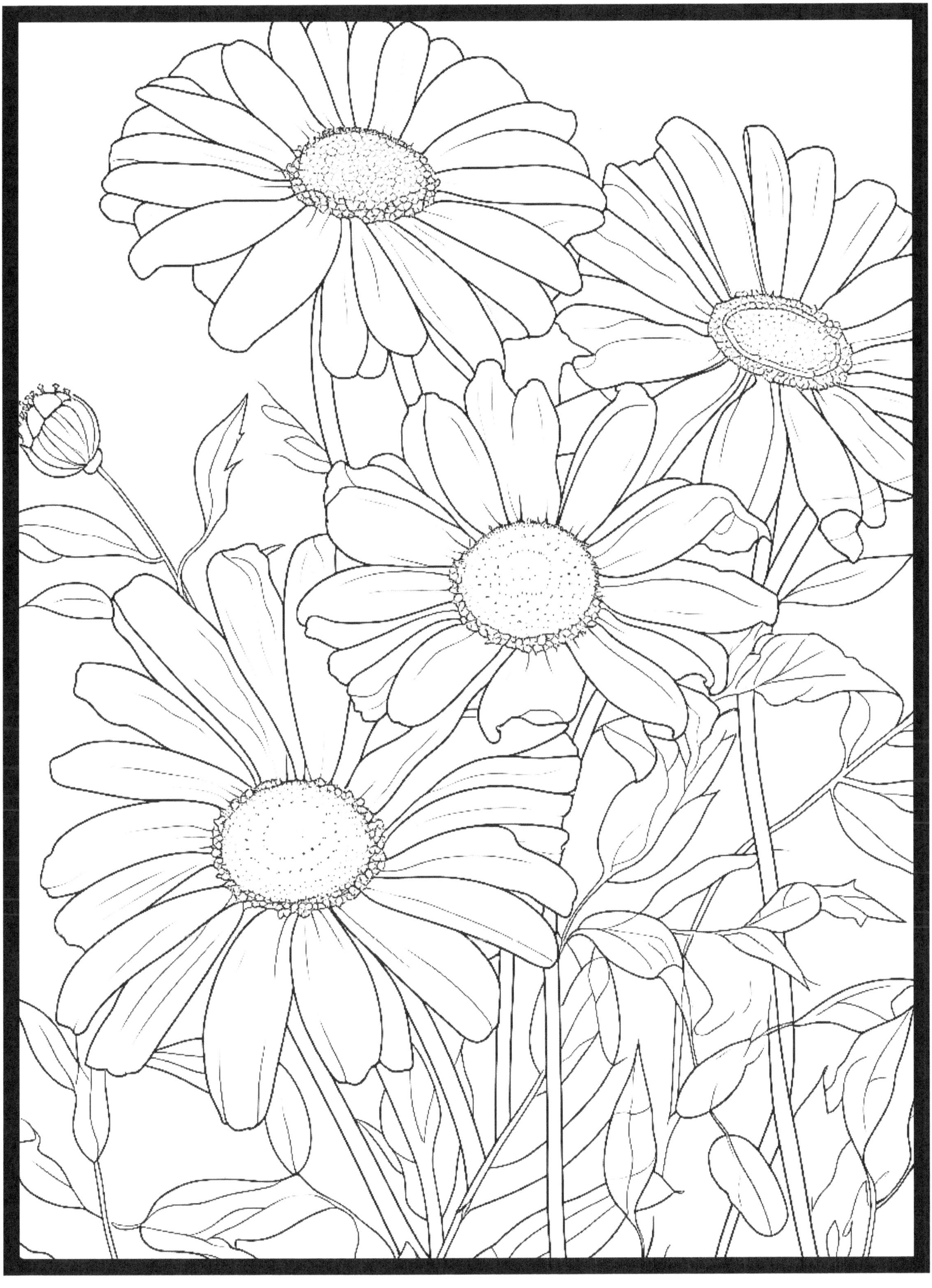

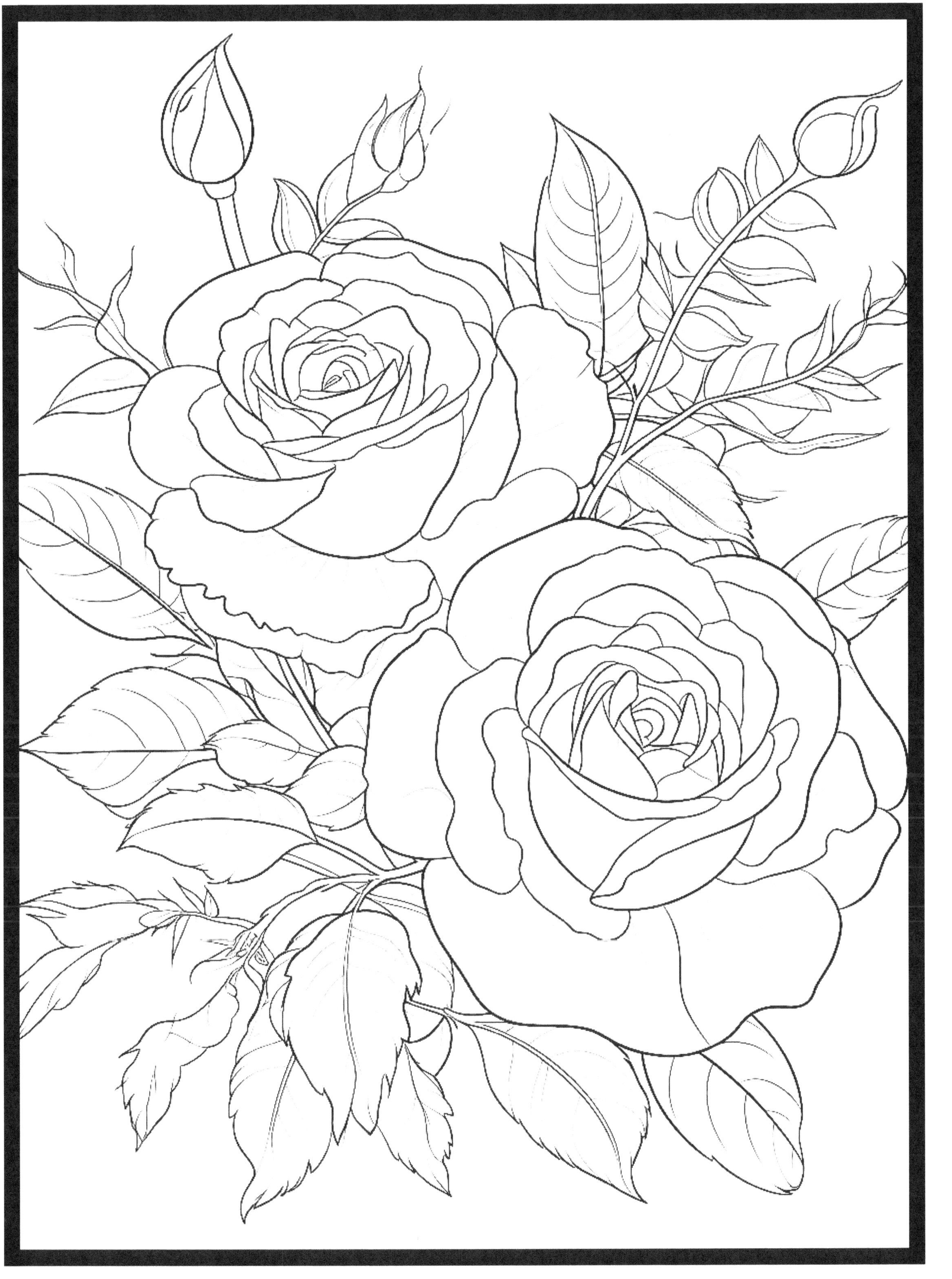

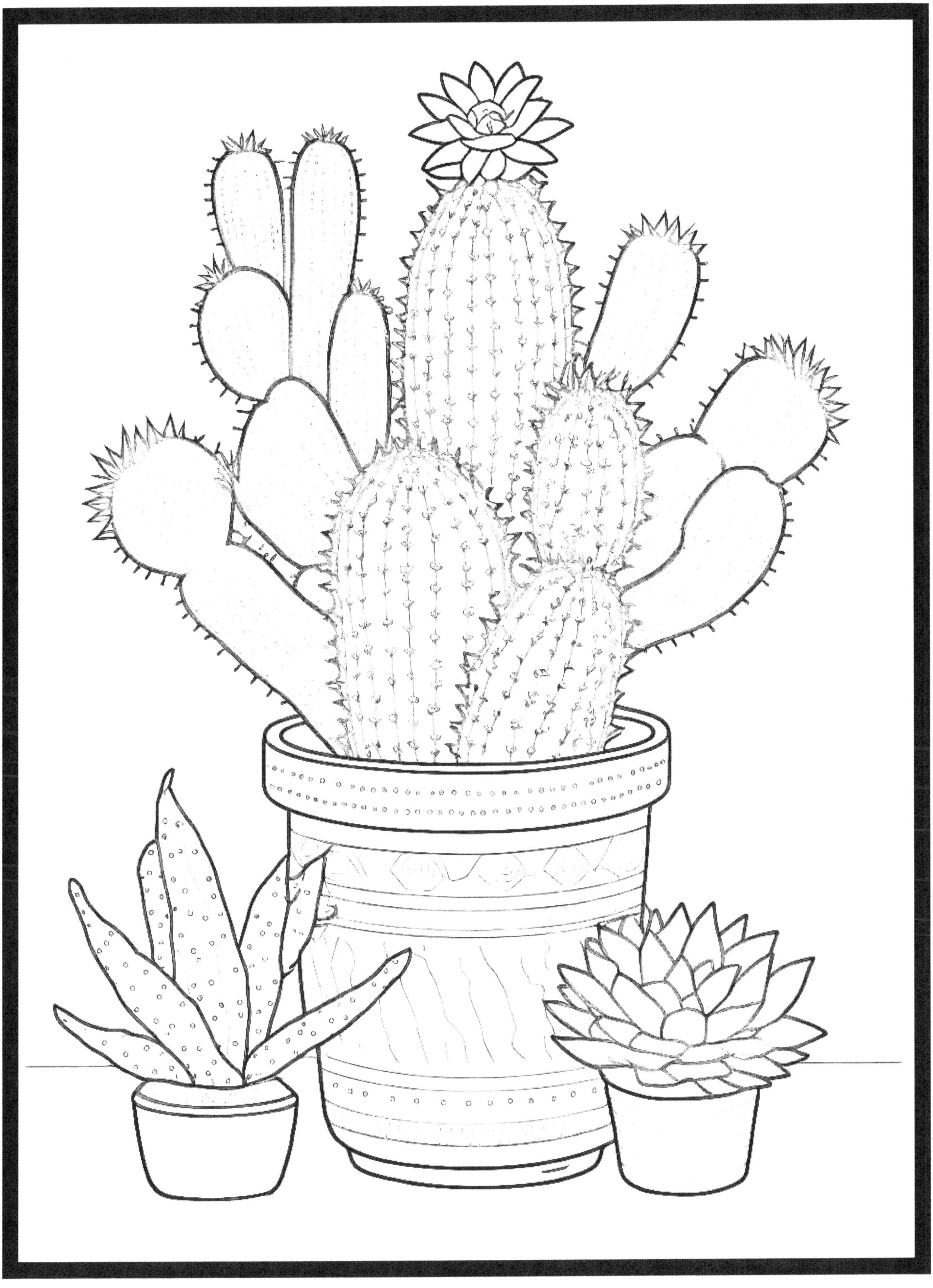

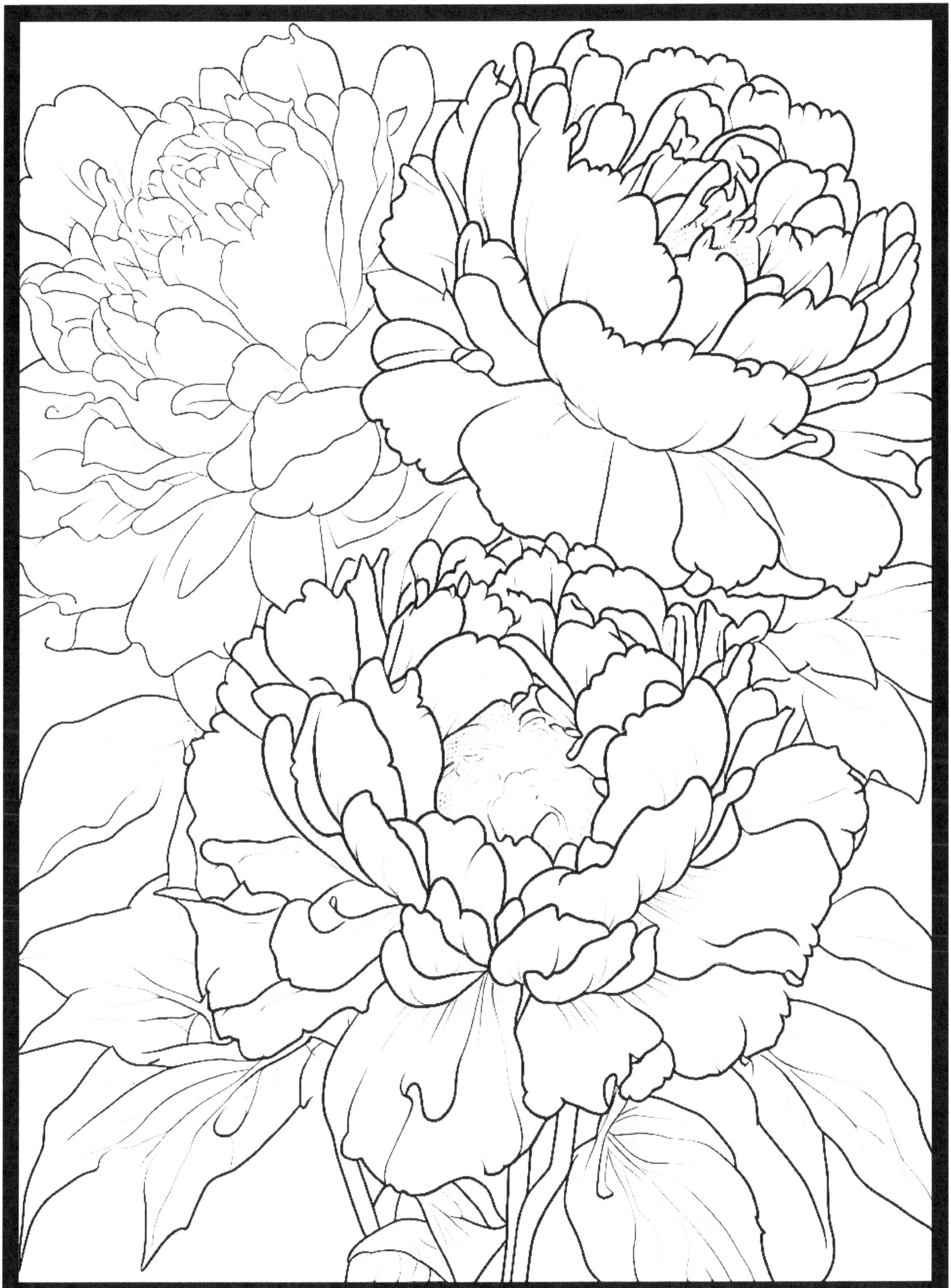

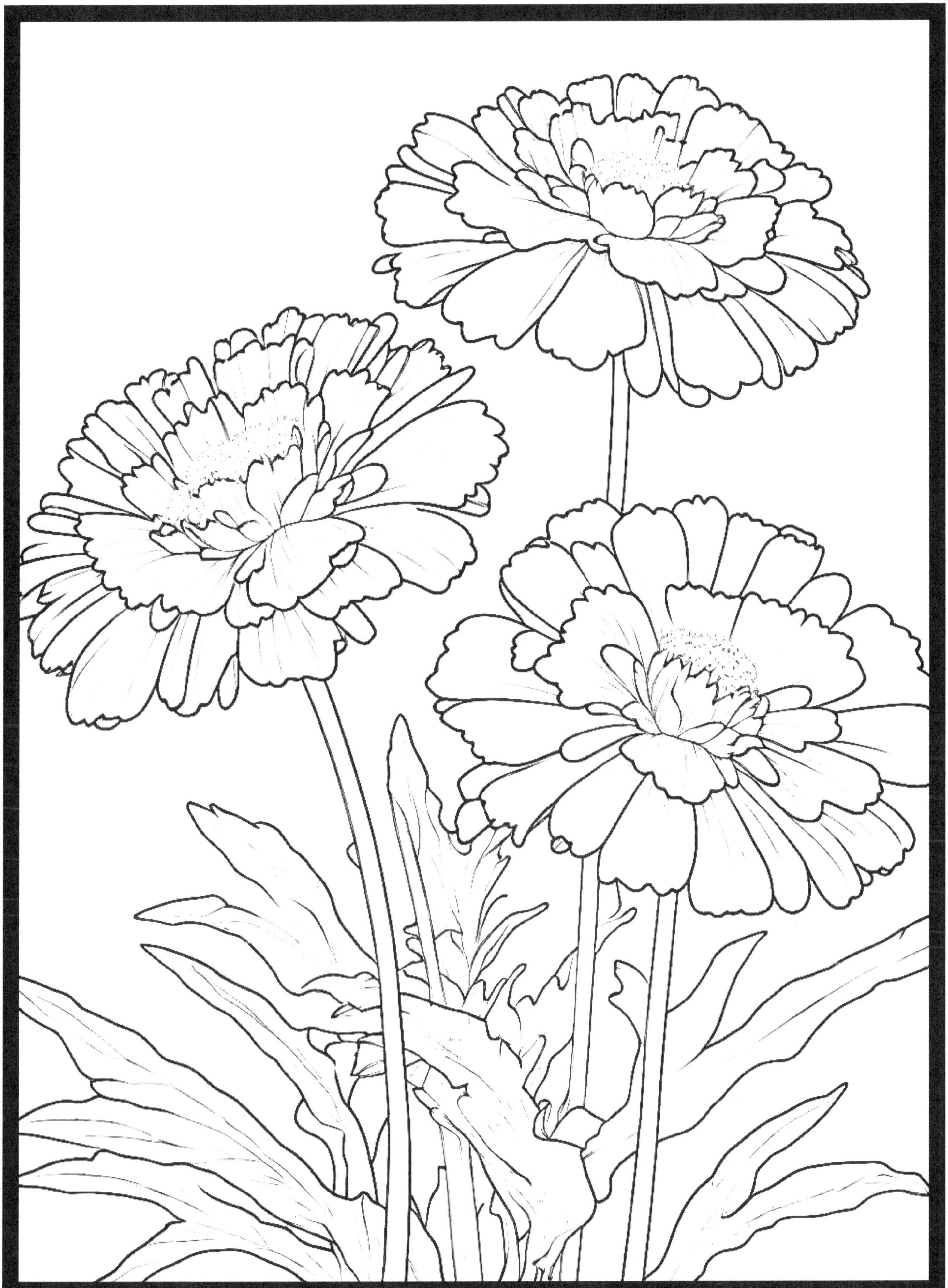

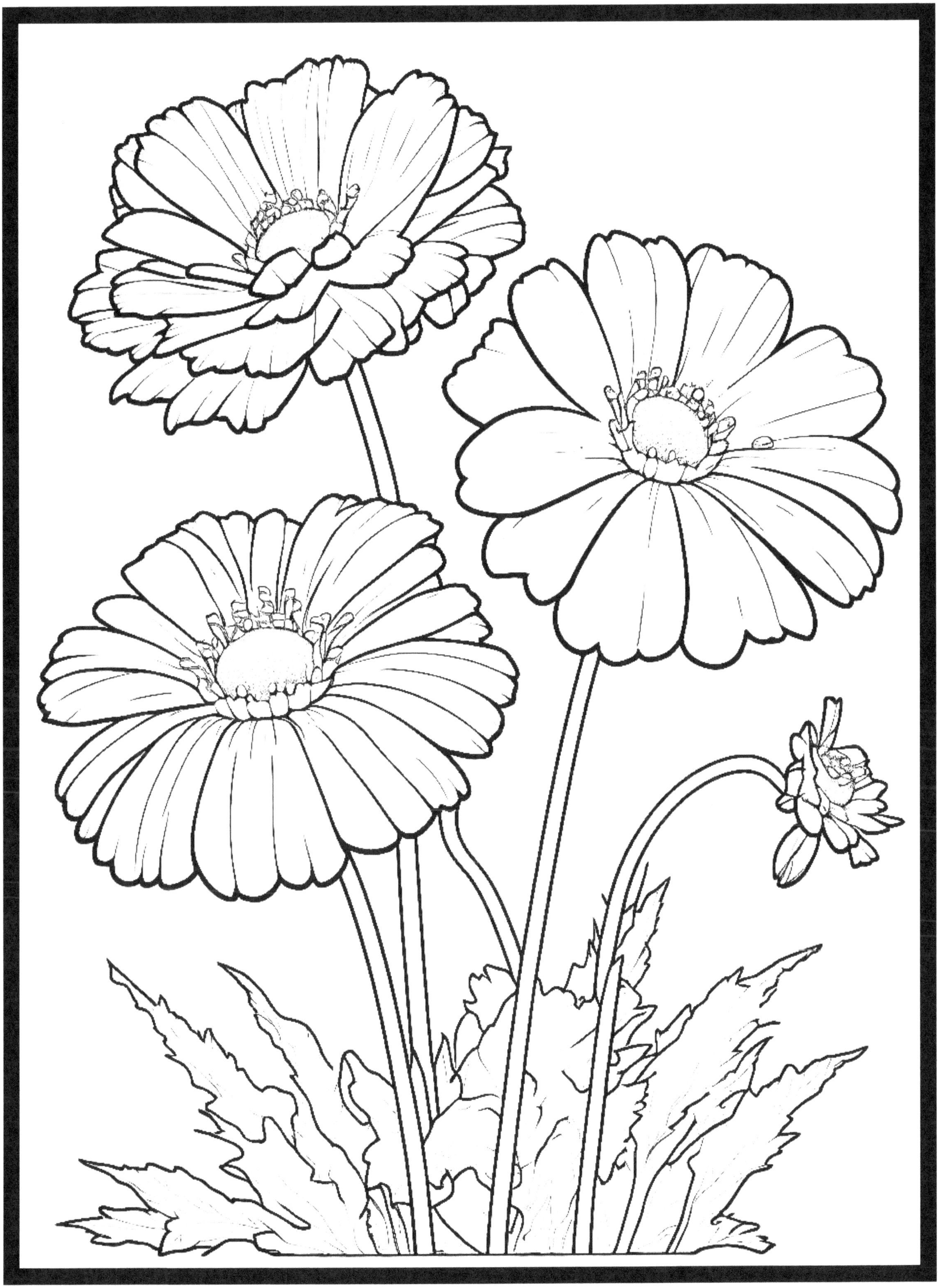

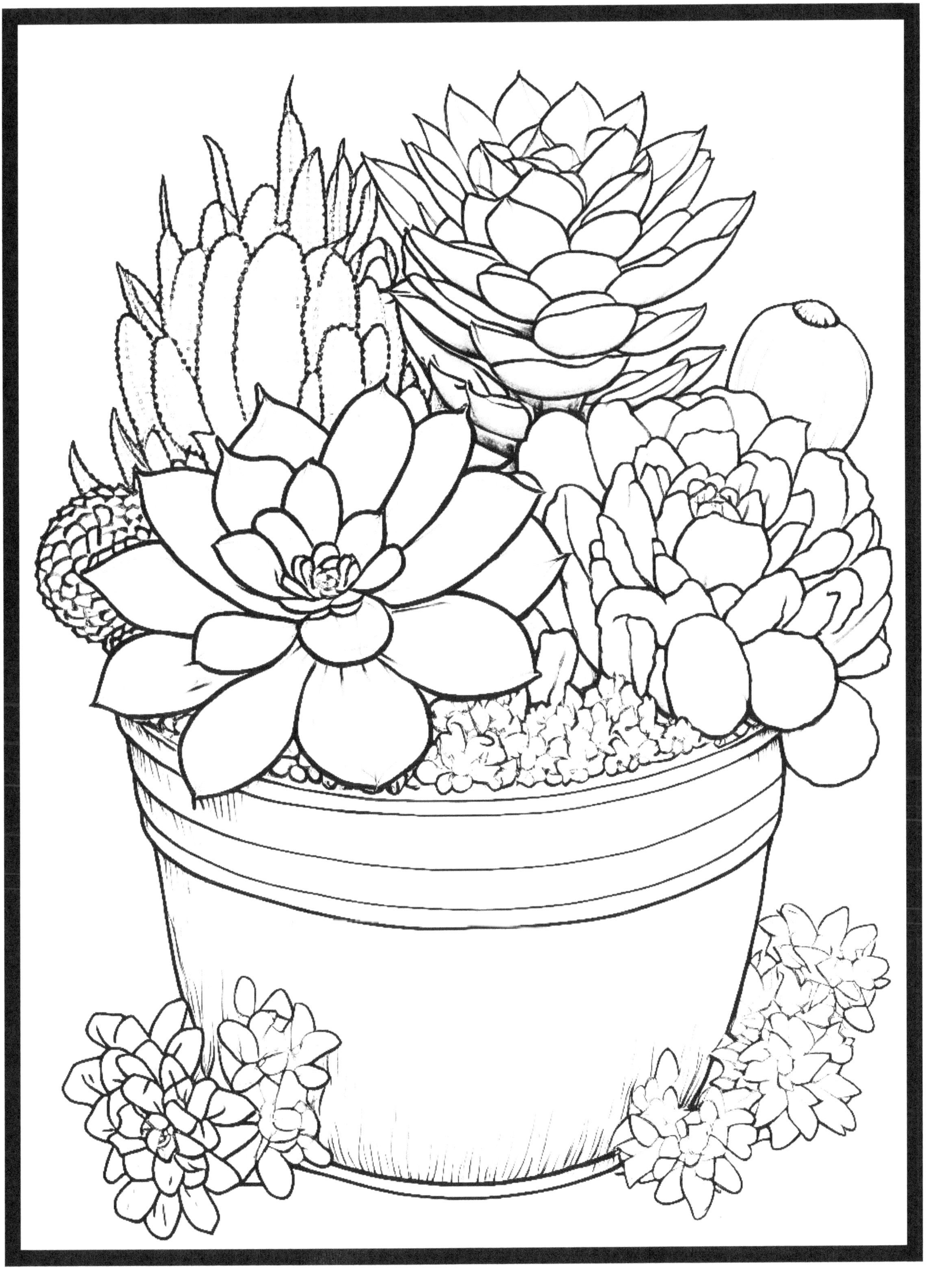

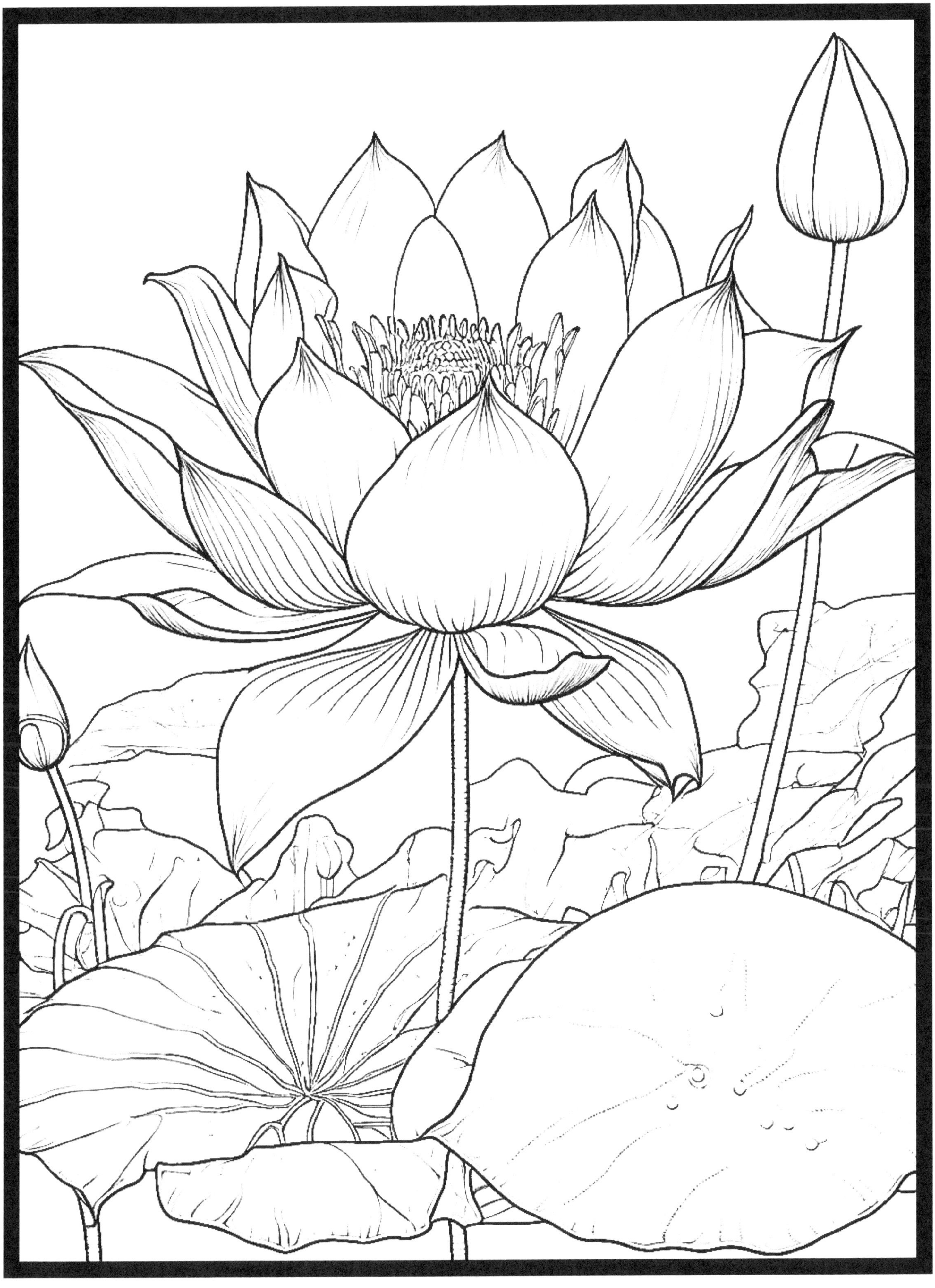

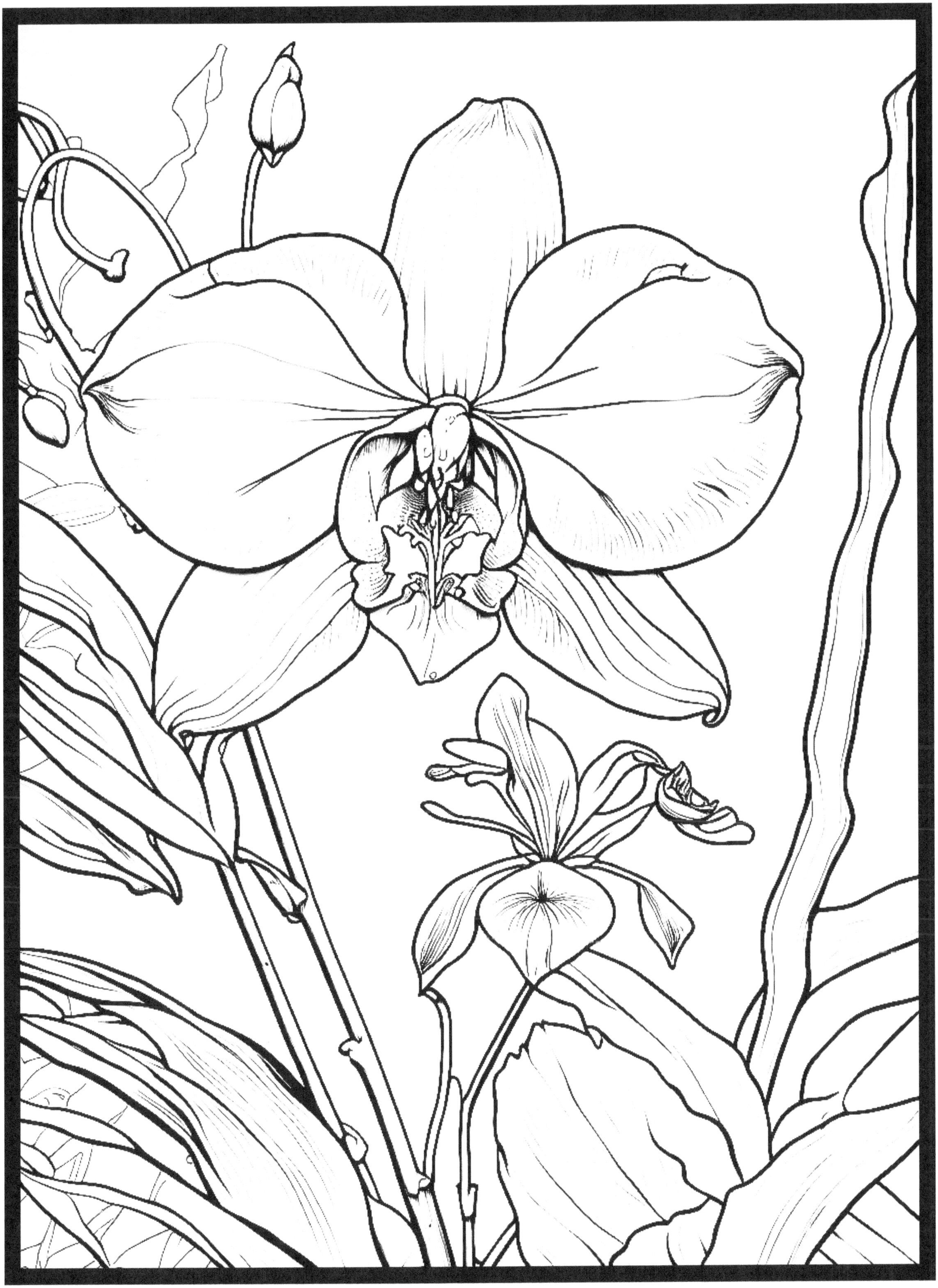

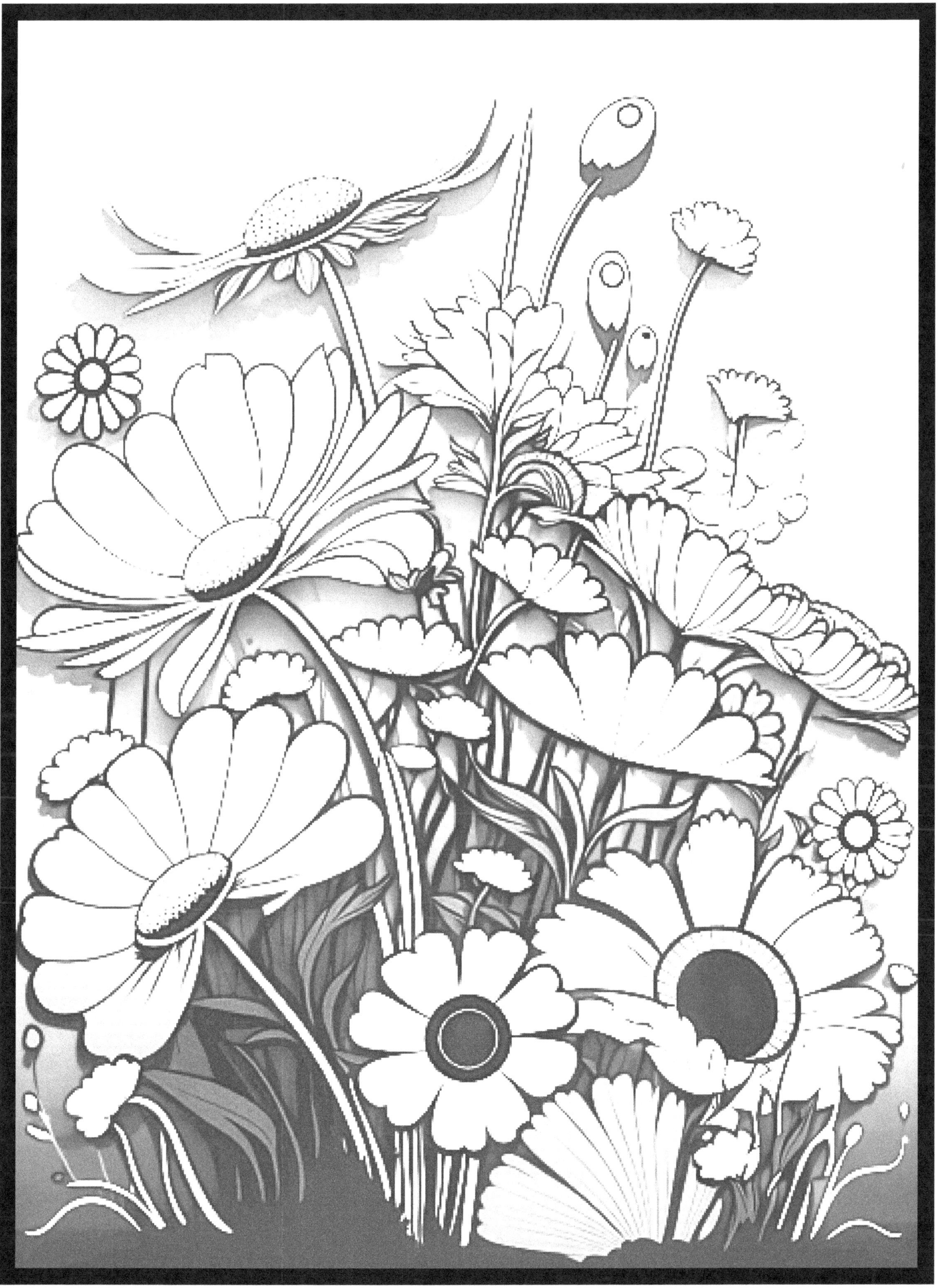

www.ingramcontent.com/pod-product-compliance
Lightning Source LLC
Chambersburg PA
CBHW082020230526
45466CB00022B/2801
* 9 7 9 8 3 9 3 3 6 9 5 7 6 *